For Skipper, Chip, Flip, and Dandelion...

AND FOR BELLA.

After Loss...

"CHOOSE LOVE."

The Heart runs deep —

and there's a part

that needs to sleep

jorever —

it will never

be OK.

(It just won't.)

(It can't.)

So —

this is dedicated to the place in your Heart that can hurt and heal and open to love again.

go outside yourself.

(where no one knows your story...
no memories to take you back.)

And see it through the good eyes of the world.

Focus on a project.

(Let it be on something you feel good about.)

Get your mind-and-body busy

to give your Heart a break.

(Give your Heart a bit of time to heal.)

Take a long walk...

(try going barefoot to feel the earth with your toes.)

Connect with the earth.

Feel your toes.

Take a long, deep breath in...

then let it out
and out
and out and out
and out.

(Do it again.)

Even for a moment,

Stop the pain.

Treat yourself
to a deliciously-long hot shower or bath

and a bar of your favorite soap.

Then

go to sleep

with a cat

curled up

against you.

When you wake up, study the lines of something beautiful.

Find words.

Find words
that touch your Heart...

and tape them
inside/outside cupboard doors
so that every time
you look at them,

you smile!

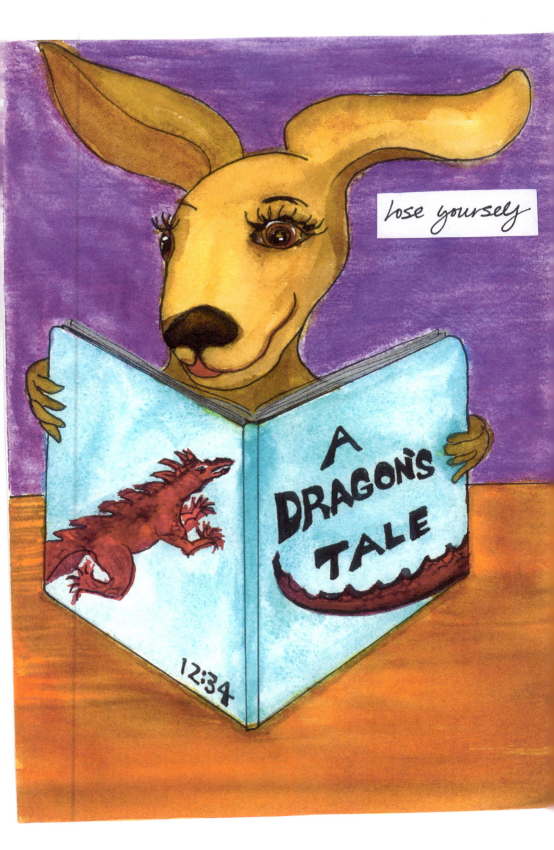

in a children's book

where magic is real

and

wishes

come

true.

**Find a rainbow in the darkness.**

Find a rainbow

in the darkness

'round the full moon

on an oh-so-cloudy night.

( Breathe in its colors...

For although

things will never be the same,

you
can
find
your
own
way
through.

Text Copyright © 2016 by Tayler K Scott
Illustrations Copyright © 2016 by Mary Lowie Kearney

All Rights Reserved

ISBN 978-1-59594-565-5

With Love from Ravenwood

Mary Lowie Kearney & Tay Scott

Published by WingSpan Press

CPSIA information can be obtained
at www.ICGtesting.com
Printed in the USA
BVHW020024101220
595299BV00001B/1